Under the Sea

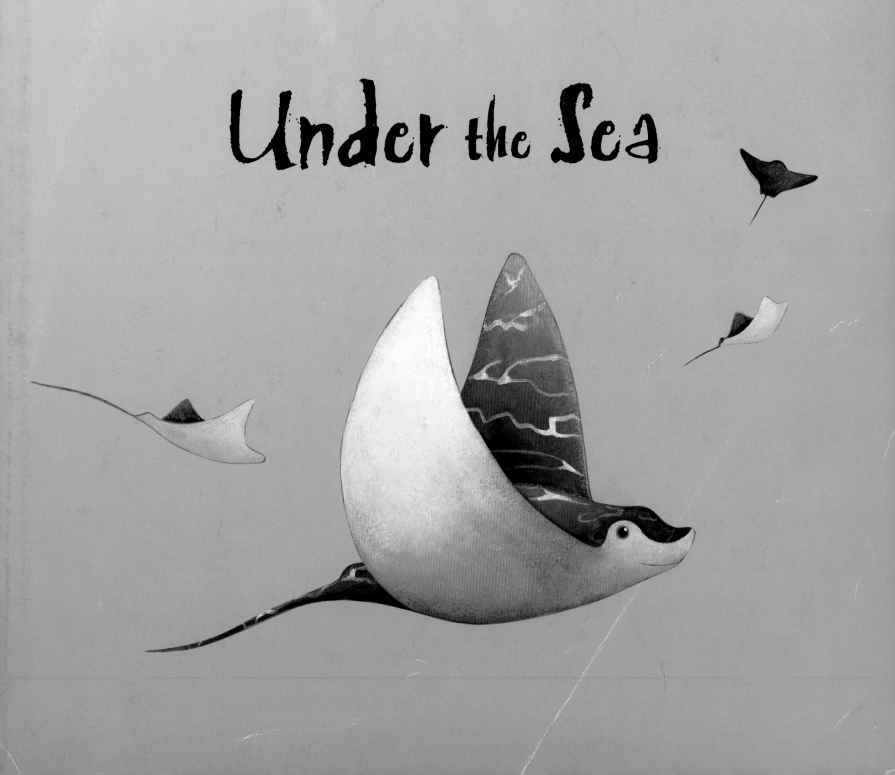

Edited by Gillian Doherty
With thanks to Dr. Margaret Rostron and
Dr. John Rostron for information about sea life.

Near a sunny shore, where the water is warm,
there are hundreds of jewel-bright fish.

They bustle around the coral reef
nibbling at teeny-tiny plants.

The sea is so big it reaches all around the world.
In each place it's as different as can be.

A hungry eel slinks out
of its hole to hunt.

Any creature it finds
might become a midnight snack!

When morning comes, the eel skulks home,
and other creatures roam around.

In an underwater meadow,
sea cows munch on long sea grass.

A group of rays
swims slowly by.

They flap their wings as though they're flying
and glide out into the open sea.

Imagine sailing across the wide, blue sea.
There's nothing but water for miles and miles.

Then suddenly beneath you swims
the **biggest** creature there's ever been.

It's a gentle giant — a big blue whale.
He's searching for other whales.

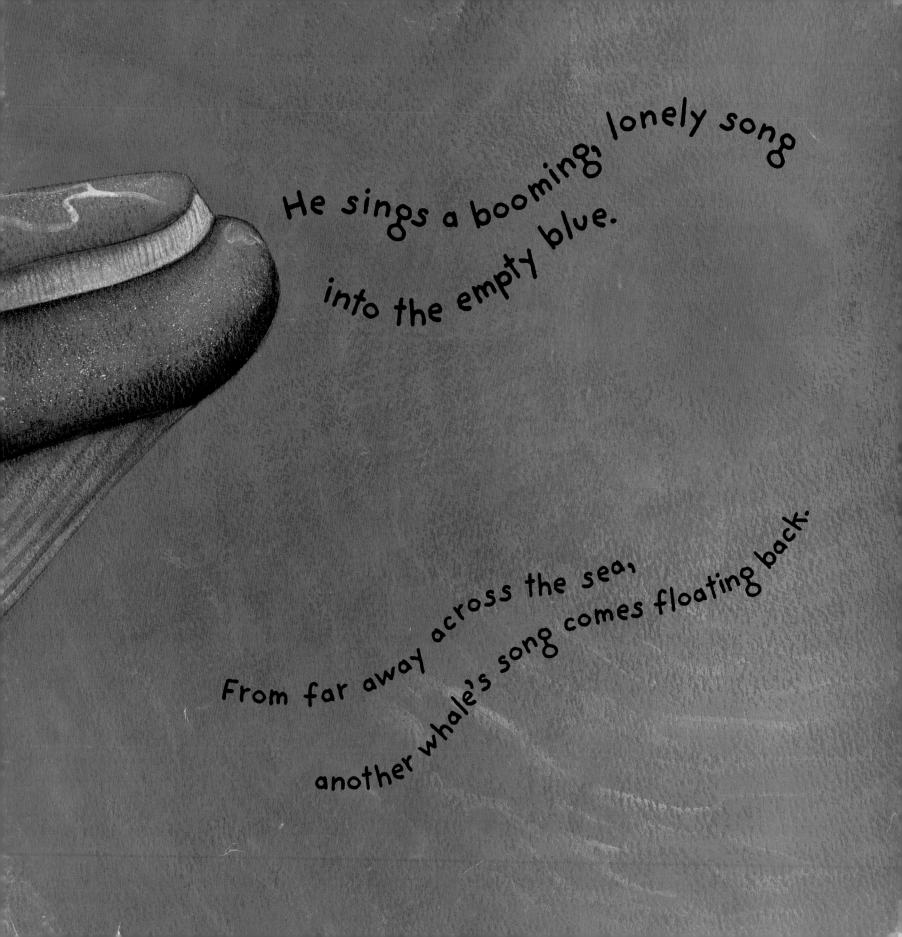

He sings a booming, lonely song
into the empty blue.

From far away across the sea,
another whale's song comes floating back.

Out here, far from any shore, the sea is VERY deep.

It gets darker and darker
the deeper you go.

Then, all at once,
twinkling lights appear.

All kinds of strange and pretty creatures are flashing messages in the dark.

It takes hours to get
to the bottom of the sea.

People have been there
in little submarines.

They found mountains and valleys,
just like you see on land.

But there were other things
no one had ever seen before.

Odd, rocky chimneys
puff out hot, black water...

and pearly crabs
and scarlet tubeworms
live all around.

Not many things live at the bottom of the sea.
Most live near the top, where it's sparkling-bright.

Tumbling schools of silvery fish
rush along beneath the waves.

Dolphins chase after them,
rounding up the fish to eat.

Dolphins can't breathe underwater
like all the fishes do.

They have to breathe the air instead,
through little blowholes on their heads.

They leap out of the water as they speed along,
and catch a breath before they dive back down.

You could spend forever and a day
exploring the deep, blue sea.

But sail far enough across the waves
and you'll always come to shore.